I lost Buck this morning. He died, I didn't cry.

I don't know why.

I found him one late night when I was reading. I heard a sound of a puppy crying.

I came out of my house and found a cute, fat little puppy.

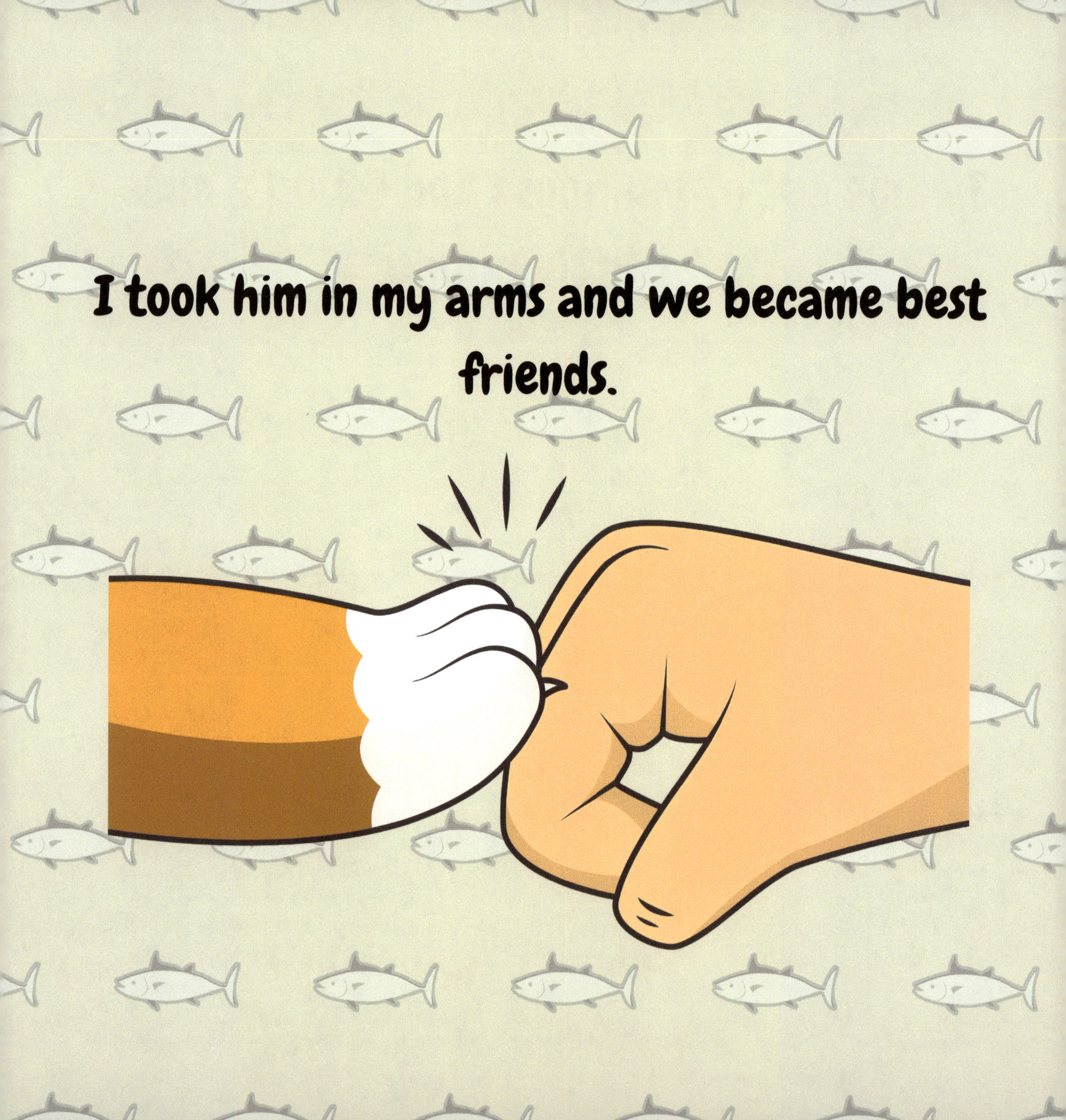
I took him in my arms and we became best friends.

From that day Buck was staying in my room.

As time passed, we became inseparable.

Meanwhile Buck had grown much bigger and I had to move him to a doghouse.

I still remember the times when Buck kept staring at me.

He looked very prudent as if he was staring at my soul

Whenever I saw him like that, I would hug him dearly

At night I used to walk with him
looking at the stars

I know very well that Buck also loved me.

He made me laugh whenever we played with a ball.

The only thing he could do was to fetch the ball after I threw it.

We used to go everywhere together.

Now I lost my Buck, with whom I shared many unforgettable memories

I miss how he greeted me by lifting a paw.

I miss his gentle smile.

I miss his cuddling when I am asleep in the morning.

It feels like I have lost a part of me.

Now that he is not with me,

I keep remembering all these memories.

I feel so empty when I look at the sky.

Why he had to go away leaving me?

But I am sure he is in a good place.

He is with God and I know he will be okay.

So I need to be strong too.

I know it will be hard.

And I know Buck will also be happy.

I will move on.

But I will never forget him.

Because he is my first ever best friend.

www.ingramcontent.com/pod-product-compliance
Lightning Source LLC
Chambersburg PA
CBHW042114110726
48006CB00002B/633
9798828368570